# Colonel Daniel Putnam's Letter Relative to the Battle of Bunker Hill and General Israel Putnam

# COLONEL DANIEL PUTNAM'S LETTER

## RELATIVE TO THE

## BATTLE OF BUNKER HILL

### AND

## GENERAL ISRAEL PUTNAM

[In this article the notes, with one exception, were all written by the author.]

*To the President and Directors of the Bunker Hill Monument Association.*

THE account published in 1818 of the battle of Bunker Hill, and especially the charges which it contained against the character of the late Major General Israel Putnam, has led to a critical examination of the subject; and the further this examination has been pursued, the greater has the public interest been excited to elicit the truth, and the whole truth, concerning it

For almost half a century the interesting details of the first considerable battle fought in our great revolutionary contest, and, considered in all its bearings. perhaps second to none which succeeded it, were very imperfectly known to the generation which has since risen up, and they seem to have been almost as little understood by some who were actors in the tragic scenes they have endeavoured to portray

Far from my heart lies the wish to revive any of the unpleasant feelings which a former controversy may have

kindled, for of all others, the friends of Genl. Putnam
have least cause to regret the investigation that has already
taken place:—they fear not that it should be continued,
but it is their earnest desire that it may be pursued until
every truth which has any bearing on the transactions of
the 17th of June, 1775, may be as fully developed as the
nature of the case will now admit.  Too long has this important subject slumbered in obscurity,—so long that the
door of access for information from the projectors of the
enterprise, and the chief actors in it, is now forever closed
by death.

But the Bunker Hill Monument Association, which num-
bers on its roll some of the master spirits of the age, may
redeem in part the time that has been lost, by examining,
and giving to every sort of attainable evidence the weight
it deserves.  And, while I acknowledge with gratitude the
respect that has been manifested for the memory of Genl.
Putnam, by the kind attentions bestowed on his son, and
feel myself bound to avoid every thing having a tendency
to disquiet the public mind, I hope not to be thought un-
reasonably officious in addressing a communication to the
*Government of the Association.*

There are some facts relating to Genl. Putnam that have
been misstated and ought to be corrected; and there are
also many incidents calculated to shed light on his character, and particularly as it is connected with a transaction
which it may be the business of the future historian to in-
vestigate and settle,—that are known perhaps to no one
now living but myself.  The years I have already numbered admonish me that many more are not to be expected, and that this may be the only opportunity I shall
ever have to record them

Little respect is due to a son who feels regardless of his
father's good name; and the confession shall not be withheld, that I am ready to sacrifice every thing but *truth* to
this paramount object.  I make this remark, that those

who read it may understand my feelings and make such
allowance as they see fit, for any of the statements which
may follow.

Whoever has lived sixty-five years, and will look back
to events which occurred at the age of fifteen or sixteen,
tho' they may be the ordinary events of common life, he
will yet find them more distinctly impressed on his memory
than those of a later period; but, if they have in them any
thing new or uncommon,—if they differ essentially in
their magnitude or importance from such as had ordin-
arily occurred in his own sphere of life, they become
indelible.

Translated from the plough in April 1775 to the head
quarters of a popular general officer, and remaining there
till the March following, the change in my condition
was great, though that general was my father, and the im-
pressions left of passing events can hardly fail to be abiding.
Having little to do but to see, and hear, and treasure up
in my mind, the sayings and doings of others,—with daily
opportunities also of witnessing the familiar interchange of
sentiments and opinions of distinguished men, and having
besides the advantage of learning from my father every
thing he knew, that was proper for a youth of my age to
know,—I must have been an arrant blockhead not to have
understood pretty well the general history of the campaign
of '75, without any subsequent helps. But, when it is considered that for the four succeeding years I was with him
in the army, and most of that time in his military family,
as his aid,—and that till the day of his death, more than
fifteen years after, was constantly near him, I must have
had abundant opportunity of knowing all that he could
communicate on the subject.

A careful retrospection, I hope, has enabled me to
relate some incidents that may be interesting at this
time, and assist the future historian in his search after
truth; and I most respectfully ask, that this statement

may be permitted to remain on the files of the Association, with any other evidence it may be thought proper to preserve. It is also my intention to send a duplicate to the Historical Society lately incorporated at Hartford in this State.

In Mr. Bradford's account of the battle of Bunker Hill, recently published in Boston, although the character of Genl. Putnam is treated respectfully, and no improper motives are attributed to the author,—yet, there is a note on the 9th page which requires explanation. Speaking of Genl. Putnam he says, "though *called General*, he had *then*" (at the time of the battle,) "command only of a Regiment." Now if the fact was indeed so,—that Putnam had no rank above that of Colonel, and that he was only "called General" by courtesy, as the writer seems to intimate, well may the claim, which he always maintained from the time of the battle till the day of his death, that he was appointed to, and did in fact exercise command from the first occupancy of the hill, until they were driven from it by the point of their enemies bayonets,—well, I say, may such a claim be disputed, for there were other colonels engaged, and their "relative rank" had not been settled  Probably Mr. Bradford's error originated from circumstances which it may not be improper to relate at this time

A few yet living remember that some time before the battle of Lexington,* the people of Connecticut were alarmed

---

* Saturday, September 3d, 1774, the report of the seizure of the powder at Quarry Hill, by order of General Gage, reached Pomfret "with the addition, that the British troops and men-of-war had fired on the people of Boston, and killed six men at the first shot"  Messengers were immediately dispatched to summon the militia of the neighboring towns  and so promptly was the call responded to that Putnam and his committee wrote to Boston, on Monday,  But for counter intelligence, we should have had forty thousand men, well equipped and ready to march this morning"—Bancroft's History, VII, 120, 121  The following characteristic note (now in the possession of Mr Brinley) was addressed by Putnam to Colonel Godfrey Malbone, of New-

with a report that the "Regulars" had left Boston, and
were marching through the country in hostile array. This
report came, as it were, on the wings of the wind, and spread
like wildfire over the country: none stopped to trace its
source, for every one was in motion for other purposes.
Old men were mounted to spread the alarm that the "Phil-
istines were coming:"—the militia men, without waiting to
transfer their flocks and herds to their wives' and children's
care, slung the powder-horn over their shoulders, and ran
in haste with their muskets to meet on *training ground*, and
every "minute man" was at his rendezvous. Nearly the
whole population east of Connecticut River, capable of
bearing arms, held them in their hands; and simultaneously
looking forward for a leader, with one heart and one voice,
Col. Israel Putnam was proclaimed their *General;* and
notices to this effect flowed in upon him from every quarter
after the alarm, (made probably to try the spirit of the
country,) had subsided.

It was from such authority that the title of *General* was
first conferred on Col. Putnam, and it was reciprocally kept in
view, by those who gave, and him who accepted it, until
the decisive moment arrived which called him from his
plough to join the patriot host at Cambridge. When this
time came, he loitered not, but left *me*, the driver of his team,
to unyoke it in the furrow, and not many days after to follow him to camp

I have been circumstantial in this relation, because it is

---

port, (then at Pomfret, where he had a large estate) immediately after receiv-
ing the report from Boston.

'SATURDAY, 12 P M

DEAR SIR I have this minute had an express from Boston that the fight
between Boston and the Regulars [began] last night at sunset, and the cannon began to and continued playing all night, and they beg for help,—and
don't you think *it is time to go ?*

I am, Sir, your most obedient servant,

ISRAEL PUTNAM

To Col Malbone "                                    [*Pub Com* ]

descriptive of the time in which it happened, and because all the particulars of it are as fresh in my recollection as if they were of yesterday. But Putnam was not long without a *legitimate* title, for before the month of April expired, (as the records of the State will shew,) he was appointed a Brigadier General, by the Assembly of the Colony, and long before the battle of Bunker Hill was in possession of his commission. Nor was it altogether correct in Mr. Bradford to state, that previous to that battle "he had command only of a Regiment."

It is true, there was at that time no other Connecticut troops at Cambridge but Putnam's regiment and two or three independent companies,—but Sargeant's regiment, posted at Inman's house, and Patterson's, still farther advanced towards Lechmere's Point, (both of Massachusetts,) were placed under his immediate orders. I know this fact, from having often myself in the night season accompanied the officers who performed the "grand rounds" for Genl. Putnam's command; and also, that the selection of officers for this duty was made alternately from those regiments and his own.

The fact may not now be generally known, but it is not the less a *truth*, that the presence of Genl. Putnam at Cambridge was extremely desirable to Genl. Ward, and it was for that reason that he was separated from the other Connecticut troops and placed near Head Quarters. His "unaccountable popularity" was not confined to Connecticut, but pervaded the whole of the Massachusetts forces then before Boston; and there was not a soldier in their ranks but seemed ready to follow him, to fight for him, and if need be to die by his side. Even Warren, the accomplished gentleman, the daring patriot, and the future hope of the army, delighted, when the complicated duties of his station permitted, to spend an hour at Putnam's quarters. He would listen attentively to his tales of a former war, and make earnest and particular enquiries of him as to the relative power and usefulness of British and Provincial troops in that war. Putnam maintained, that when the Provincial regiments were well officered, they were not inferior to the British. ' Our men," he said, "would always follow wherever their officers led,—I know this to have been the case with mine, and have also seen it in other instances." Warren asked if 10,000 British should march out of Boston, what number in his opinion would be competent to meet them? Putnam answered, let me pick my officers, and I would not fear to meet them with half the number;—not in a pitched battle to stop them at once, for no troops are better than the British, but I would fight on the retreat, and every stone wall we passed should be lined with their dead;—our men are lighter of foot, they understand our grounds and how to take advantage of them; and besides, we should only fall back on our *reserve*, while every step they advanced, the country would close on their flanks and rear.*

Until the appointment of Washington, Genl. Ward's was a delicate and highly responsible station, and it was natural he should not only wish for Genl. Putnam's experience and advice to assist him in difficulties, but that there should be one who stood high in the confidence of the people, *on* whom he might lean for support, and *with* whom he might divide the responsibility. Their views of public affairs, and the proper measures to be pursued, were not exactly the same, but the utmost harmony subsisted between them. The predominant *wish* of that time was "peace and reconciliation,"—and the prevalent *opinion*, growing out of

---

* This doctrine might have been *orthodox* in '75, while the spirit of the country was up, but it would have been heretical in '76, when the little remnant of an almost disbanded army worn out with fatigue and spiritless from disaster was flying through New Jersey with their enemy at their heels, and not an arm uplifted to stay their progress. But Putnam had reference only to New England, and perhaps at no stage of the war would his position have been *very* erroneous as applied to that particular section of our country.

that wish, that Britain would relax the rigour of her measures, and a compromise be the result.  Such were the
views of Genl. Ward, but Putnam held different sentiments.
Without any wish for "reconcilation," he believed that
Britain would persevere in her demands, and that America
had no alternative but submission, or a long protracted resistance  In support of this remark, though it may be
somewhat out of place, I beg leave to relate an anecdote, of
which I was myself a witness

From the arrival of Washington at Cambridge till the
enemy left Boston, his and Putnam's families were not only
on the most friendly terms, but their intercourse was very
frequent  Not a week passed but they dined together at
the quarters of one or the other.  One day in the month of
September, Genl. Washington at his table gave for a toast,—
"*A speedy and honorable peace,*" and all appeared to join with
good will in the sentiment.   Not many days after, at Putnam's quarters, addressing himself to Washington he said,—
"Your Excellency, the other day, gave us "a speedy and
honorable peace," and I, as in duty bound, drank it, and
now, I hope Sir, you will not think it an act of insubordi-
nation if I ask you to drink one of rather a different character  I will give you, Sir, "*A long and a moderate war.*"   It
has been truly said of Washington, that he seldom smiled
and almost never laughed, but the sober and sententious
manner in which Putnam delivered his sentiment, and its
seeming contradiction to all his practice, came so unexpect-
edly on Washington that he did laugh, more heartily than
I ever remember to have seen him before or after; but presently he said, "You are the last man Genl. Putnam from
whom I should have expected such a toast, you who are all
the time urging vigorous measures, to plead now for a *long*,
and, what is still more extraordinary, a *moderate* war, seems
strange indeed."   Putnam replied, that "the measures he
advised were calculated to prevent, not hasten, a peace,
which would be only a *rotten thing*, and last no longer than

it divided us. I expect nothing but a *long* war, and I would have it a *moderate* one, that we may hold out till the mother country becomes willing to cast us off forever." Washington did not soon forget this toast, for years after, and more than once, he reminded Putnam of it. But let me return from this digression to my narrative.

In the month of May, an armed vessel of the enemy was destroyed near Chelsea, by a party under Genl. Putnam's command, and when he returned to his quarters, wet, and covered to the waist with marsh mud, contracted by wading over the flats to burn the vessel, he met there Genl. Ward and Dr. Warren. Without changing his dress, he related to them the events of the day, and added, "I wish we could have something of this kind to do every day, it would teach our men how little danger there is from cannon balls, for tho' they have sent a great many at us, nobody has been hurt by them." "I would," he continued, "that Gage and his troops were within our reach, for we would be like hornets about their ears; as little birds follow and teaze the eagle in his flight, we would every day contrive to make them uneasy." Warren smiled and said nothing, but Genl. Ward replied, "As peace and reconciliation is what we seek for, would it not be better to act only on the defensive, and give no unnecessary provocation?" Putnam turned to Warren and said with emphasis,—"*You know,* Dr. Warren, we shall have no peace worth any thing, till we gain it by the sword." Instead of any direct reply, Warren observed—"Your wet clothes must be uncomfortable, General, and we will take our leave that you may change them,"—and taking Putnam's hand, he continued, "I admire your spirit and respect Genl. Ward's prudence,—both will be necessary for us, and one must temper the other."

Frequent interviews of this sort happened between these and other officers at Putnam's quarters, which was at Borland's house, and being central was a common resort

for the higher officers of the army, as well as the leading
characters in civil affairs.   Putnam's regiment, which had a
partial supply of tents, was encamped on the high ground
near Phipps' house, and a considerable share of the men
were every day employed in throwing up redoubts, called
No. 1, and No 2, for besides their usefulness for defence if
the enemy should advance in that direction, Putnam's experience had taught him that raw and undisciplined troops
*must* be employed in some way or other, or they would
soon become vicious and unmanagible.   His maxim was,
"It is better to dig a ditch every morning and fill it up at
evening than to have the men idle."

One afternoon, as Putnam had been marking out a new
line on which his men had just commenced work, Col.
Prescott and Col. Gardner came up, " I wish General, said
Prescott, your men were digging nearer Boston "   Putnam
replied that he wished so too, and hoped ere long we should
all be of one mind.

About this time an exchange of prisoners took place at
Charlestown, where Genl. Putnam was present in behalf of
the army, and Dr. Warren, as the head of the civil depart-
ment.   Putnam returned to his quarters in high spirits,—
said he had met again some of his old friends, but appeared
most gratified that Gage should have consented to an exchange of prisoners.   "He may *call* us *Rebels*, now, if he
will. but why then don't he hang his prisoners instead of
exchanging them?   By this act he has virtually placed us
on an equality, and acknowledged our *right* of resistance."
Next day there was quite a *levee* of officers at Putnam's
quarters to talk about the exchange, etc.   He related to
them all the particulars, and turning to Col. Prescott, said,
"Colonel, I saw ground yesterday that may suit your
purpose, I suppose you have not forgotten your remark of the other day, about *digging;* but more of
this another time."   Prescott called in the evening, and
they walked out together, for several succeeding days

he was at Putnam's quarters, and they were in private conversation.

After a while, nearly all the troops quartered at Cambridge were ordered to parade on the common, armed and accoutred. My name had been entered on the roll of Genl. Putnam's company as a volunteer, and on some occasions I took my station in the ranks, this was one of them, and I felt proud to be numbered among what I then thought a mighty host destined for some great enterprize. We were marched to Charlestown, and I supposed it was intended to "take Boston," but, after parading about on the high grounds awhile, we all returned in safety to our quarters at Cambridge.

For several days after, Genl. Putnam appeared thoughtful and absent in his mind. In such seasons of abstraction he was in the habit of giving an indistinct kind of utterance to his thoughts,—or what may be termed *"talking to one's self,"* and broken sentences, such as follow, escaped his lips,—"We must go there,"—"Think they will come out,"—"Yes, yes, they must,"—"I'll go with my regiment any how,"—"We must go in the night,"—"We'll carry our tools and have a trench before morning,"—"He's a good fellow,"—"He wants to go,"—"Says he will go, if they'll let him,"—"Lay still—*lay still I say*, till they come close,"—"They wont hurt you,"—"I know 'em of old, they fire without aim,"—these and such like burstings of his mind continued several days,—not in a regular chain as I have set them down, but breaking forth occasionally, and often accompanied with some significant gesture, which left no doubt but he was contemplating some important military operation. To *me* it was almost certain, for I had all my life been accustomed to such sallies, but more especially after the *alarm* before related, up to the affair at Lexington, he had almost daily such like communings with himself

Mr Inman, besides being a timid man, prone to seek his

own safety, was also "a friend of government," and on
the day of Lexington battle retired to Boston, leaving his
house and farm to the management of his wife, who had
several young ladies residing with her. The soldiers had
committed some depredations on her property, and fearing
personal insult, she applied to Genl Putnam for protection.
Sargeant's regiment was quartered in the out buildings on
the farm, but for greater security of the family, by direction of my father I had from about the middle of May,
lodged every night in her house, and young as I was, the
family confided much in the protection afforded by ' General Putnam's son "

The day before the battle of Bunker Hill, I noticed an
unusual stir among the troops at Cambridge. Putnam's
regiment was under arms, and I was informed by the Adjutant that a detachment had been made from it for "secret
service;" but what at the time impressed my mind most
strongly, was the preparation my father himself was making. With his own hands he prepared cartridges for his
pistols,—took out the old flints and put in new. While he
was doing this, Col Prescott came in, and observing what
he was about, said in a low tone, I see General, *you* are
making preparation, and *we* shall be ready at the time A
little after sunset my father called me aside, and said, "You
will go to Mis Inman's as usual tonight, and it is time
you were gone. You need not return here in the morning, but stay there tomorrow; the family may want you,
and if they find it necessary to leave the house, you must
go with them where they go; and try now my son, to be
as serviceable to them as you can." This order, connected
with what I had seen during the day, left no doubt in my
mind that some military movement was going forward in
which my father was to participate. I called to mind his
abstraction and self-communing,—the broken sentences
that had escaped him, indicating battle and bloodshedding,
and my imagination pictured him as mangled with wounds

and none to help him. With earnest entreaty, I asked leave to accompany him.—"*You, dear father,*" I said, "may need my assistance *much more* than Mrs. Inman; *Pray* let me go where you are going." "No, no, Daniel,—do as I have bid you," was the answer, which he affected to give sternly, while his voice trembled and his eyes filled. Then as if perfectly comprehending what had been passing in my mind, he added, "You can do little my son, where I am going, and besides, there will be enough to take care of me." I went as directed to Mrs. Inman's, but took no interest in the conversation of her nieces, or the maternal kindness of their aunt: my mind was elsewhere, and I retired early to bed, but not to sleep: the night was as sleepless to me as to those who were toiling or watching on the confines of Boston. I had a strong suspicion that Charlestown was the spot to which the hostile movement was directed; and long before the first gun fired, had risen and seated myself at the window of my chamber, anxiously looking thitherward.

The cannonade which commenced early, and seemed every moment to increase, soon brought the family together in terror and amazement. Mrs Inman's first request to me was "Pray don't leave *us* till you hear from your father." I told her, from what I had seen the day before, and my father's direction to me at parting, I could hardly expect to hear from him that day, and might *never* hear more from him while he lived. I then repeated to her the order my father had given me and the request I had made of him, adding (as well as my emotions would allow me to add,) "and now, my dear madam, though my heart and soul must be with *him*, I will stay with and do all in my power to assist *you*." She clasped me in her arms and exclaimed, "Oh happy General Putnam in such a son,—happy youth in possession of so good a mind!" And from that moment to the end of her life, which was not till a number of years after the war had closed, she manifested for me all the

kindness and affection which the exclamation of that
moment indicated  There is *one** besides myself yet
living who will remember how unmeasured that kindness was

Upon my promise of returning immediately, Mrs Inman
consented that I should run to my father's quarters, and
learn if possible where he was, and what might be the expected result of the cannonade, which had now become
tremendous.  On my way I passed the encampment of
Genl. Putnam's Regt. which was under arms, and observing
Major Durkee in front, I asked him if he knew where I
could find my father?  He seemed for a moment lost at
such a question from me, but presently, pointing his sword
towards Charlestown, he said, "Where yonder cannon roar,
—where else would you expect to find him?"  I pressed
forward to Genl. Putnam's quarters, where I found the
adjutant of his regiment, who informed me the General
had been there, but for a moment, and had returned to
Charlestown as soon as the firing began.  Not satisfied
with this, I walked on to Genl Ward's quarters.  The
General had gone out, but I found his secretary, Mr Joseph
Ward, who appeared a good deal confused and agitated.
He immediately asked if "I did not think the British would
be in Cambridge before night," and added, "Your father
was here before dawn of day this morning, and has gone
back to Charlestown."  I asked if Genl Ward had gone
there also?  "No, but he has gone to send a reinforcement to your father '  (This was probably between eight
and nine in the morning.)  Returning to Mrs. Inman's, I remained there in anxious suspense, till we saw
Charlestown in flames, and heard an incessant roar of
musketry.

Mrs Inman had been all day expecting the British
would embark troops from the bottom of the common in

---

*Mrs Judge Robbins.

Boston, and land them near where the Lexington detachment was landed, and her attention had been chiefly directed to that quarter, but the furious discharge of musketry
made it evident they had gone out some other way, and
were engaged in a battle, the issue or consequences of
which could not be foreseen.  The day was drawing towards
its close, and dreading the horrors that might overwhelm
her family in the night, every thing was put in requisition
for a hasty removal,—but it was after sunset, and not until
it had been ascertained at Cambridge that the British had
gained possession of Charlestown heights, with a loss on
both sides that none pretended to calculate, that we passed
through the scene of confusion there visible, on our way to
*Brush Hill*, now the residence of Judge Robbins.  We
were hastily and but imperfectly accoutred for the jaunt,
so that it was midnight before we reached our destination.
On the way, we learned from people who passed us (some
of whom had been in the battle, or claimed to have been
so,) that General Putnam was safe, but his escape was considered miraculous, for wonderful tales were told us of
the dangers with which he had been surrounded, and
the unconcern he appeared to feel when they were the
greatest.

I was not long next morning in retracing my steps of the
last night back to Cambridge.  Genl. Putnam was not at
his quarters: he had been there it was said for a few min-
utes only, and with fresh men was then fortifying Prospect
Hill.  There I found him about ten o'clock on the morning of the 18th June, dashing about among the workmen
throwing up intrenchments, and often placing a sod with
his own hands.  He wore the same clothes he had on when
I left him, thirty-eight hours before, and affirmed he had
neither put them off, nor washed himself since,—and we
might well believe him, for the aspect of all bore evidence
that he spoke the truth.

I joined my entreaty to the earnest request of every offi-
17

cer round him, that he would go to his quarters and take
some refreshment and rest    He enquired what had become
of Mrs. Inman?    I told him where I had left her in safety,
and we went home together.    I had often heard him relate
his adventures of a former war, and my curiosity was in-
tense to know the particulars of the late battle from an au-
thentic source

At different times, and all perhaps within a week,—all
certainly while they were fresh in his recollection, he related to me the substance of what follows.

Here let it be premised, that I will not vouch my relation shall be in his own words exactly, but only that I will
endeavour to come as near them as possible; and having
so often heard them repeated in later times, in detached
parts as conversation led to them I think there will be no
great varience from the original.    Nor will I say that the
*order* of his communications shall always be preserved, for
in some instances events may have been related before the
circumstances which led to them.    All I can promise is,
and thus much I *do* promise, that my narrative shall be
given fairly, and without in any case intentionally varying
the sense.

From the time of the exchange of prisoners, Genl. Putnam said, he had never lost sight of occupying the high
grounds at Charlestown    That he had at various times
conversed with both civil and military characters on the
subject, some of whom were in favour of the measure, but
more against it    That he had mentioned it to some of the
Committee of Safety, and to two members of Congress at
Watertown, but found little encouragement from either
That he had once pressed the consideration of the subject
upon Genl Ward, who discountenanced it, but afterwards,
at his particular request permitted him to march most of
the army from Cambridge to Charlestown, when he again
examined the ground more minutely.    That he had soon
afterwards a spirited conversation with Genl. Ward, Dr.

Warren, and Col. (or Genl.) Joseph Palmer,* a member of the Committee of Safety, who inclined to favour the measure, but Ward and Warren both opposed it, alledging that as we had no powder to spare, and no battering cannon, it would be idle to make approaches on the town.

He told them they had entirely mistaken his views,— that it was not for the purpose of battering the town, but to draw the enemy from it, where we might meet them on equal terms, and that Charlestown and Dorchester were the only points where this could be done,—that the army wished to be employed, and the country was growing dissatisfied at the inactivity of it.

It was objected again, that it might bring on a general battle, and that in our situation it was neither politick or safe to risk one. He replied, 2000 men will be enough to risk, and with that number we will go on and defend ourselves as long and as well as we can, and then give the ground.

"But, suppose your retreat should be intercepted?"

We will guard against that, and run when we can contend no longer with advantage;—we can outrun them, and behind every wall rally and oppose their progress till we join our friends again.

But, suppose the worst, suppose us hemmed in and no retreat;—we know what we are contending for,—we will set our country an example of which it shall not be ashamed, and show those who seek to oppress us what men can do who are determined to live *free* or not live at all.

Warren, he said, rose, and walked several times across the room,—leaned a few moments over the back of a chair in a thoughtful attitude, and said,—"*Almost thou persuadest*

---

* This gentleman afterwards purchased a large tract of land in this town, and in 1782, while on a visit here, he called on Genl Putnam and, recurring to the time, recapitulated to him with great minuteness the details of that conversation.

*me, General Putnam,*—but I must still think the project a
rash one.   Nevertheless, if it should ever be adopted, and the
strife becomes hard, you must not be surprised to find me
with you in the midst of it."   "I hope not Sir," said Putnam, "you are yet but a young man, and our country has
much to hope from you, both in council and in war.   It is
only a little brush we have been contemplating,—let some
of us who are older and can well enough be spared *begin*
the fray,—there will be time enough for you hereafter,
for it will not soon be ended."*

It was not long after this that a council of war, at which
Warren was present, determined to fortify Bunker Hill.
There was, Genl. Putnam said, a great deal of conversation
and debate before this determination was made, but it was
finally agreed that 2000 men should be employed in the
undertaking.   Putnam was desirous that his own regiment
should make part of the force, not so much because he
thought them better or braver men than others, but because
they were better known to each other, and were also better
equipped than any other troops at Cambridge,† but Genl.
Ward would not listen to his proposition    That regiment,
he said, had already the post of danger if the enemy should
advance on Cambridge    They were in advance, had thrown

---

* Genl Putnam, when relating this conversation observed that the fate of
Warren brought to his mind that of Lord Howe, who fell by his side 17 years
before, and to whom he had given similar advice    I asked, if he knew any
of the particulars of Warren's fate, or where, or at what time he lost his life
Nothing, he replied, except that Prescott told me he was in the redoubt brav-
ing the enemy when they stormed it —but I never saw him after we parted
before the battle began

† It may be remembered that Col Grosvenor, in a letter addressed to me and
published in 1818, speaking of the detachment from Putnam's Regt under
Knowlton at the *rail fence*, says, ' Each man was provided with *one pound
of gunpowder and forty-eight balls*   This ammunition was received however
prior to marching to Breeds Hill "   In conversation with him not long before
his death, he said that Putnam's Regt , and he believed *all* the Continental
troops, had a like supply    There is a great difference between this and a
*gill cup of powder and fifteen balls* "

up works, and ought to defend them; and he was even un-willing that *any* of that regiment should be removed from the station it occupied. Putnam, however, claimed, and *in-sisted* on having part of his regiment with him, and the de-tachment under Knowlton was made accordingly. It was further stated by Putnam, that there had been an under-standing between him and Col. Prescott, that the latter should have a part in the expedition if it should ever be undertaken. Genl. Ward was apprized of this, and Pres-cott with all his regiment was ordered on that service. The reason why the whole number contemplated for the expedi-tion was not all ordered at once, Genl. Putnam stated to be this;—it was found that intrenching tools could not be had for more than about 1000 men, and he agreed to go on with that number over night, and return in the morning for re-freshments and a reinforcement or relief for those who were expected to toil all the night,—that the day was just dawning when he returned to Cambridge for that purpose, but the furious cannonade that commenced as soon almost as he reached there, and the uncertainty whether the enemy might not even then be landing, left him only time to re-quest Genl. Ward would hasten on the troops and refresh-ments as soon as possible, while he himself galloped back to see what was doing, and contrive what was in future to be done

There was certainly a great deal of confusion at Cam-bridge, and probably some unavoidable delay in conse-quence, before the order for Col Stark to march reached him at Medford. Genl Putnam was impatient of this delay, and rode a second time to Genl. Ward's quarters, when he was informed of the order that had been sent for the New Hampshire troops to march.

(Lest this expression should be thought to imply censure of Genl Ward, it is an act of justice due his memory to state, that, although the intended reinforcement was expect-ed by Genl. Putnam from Cambridge, and to have been on

the ground early in the morning, in which case more time
might have been left to complete his preparations, yet he
was sensible of the necessity which Genl. Ward felt of pre-
serving Cambridge in a defensible state, and approved the
measure of withdrawing the New Hampshire troops from
Medford, where they could not be wanted. The chief
cause of Putnam's impatience arose from the *delay*, which
was perhaps unavoidable, as these troops were ' *destitute of
ammunition*,"—a circumstance not known probably, or not
fully considered at the time, either by Ward or Putnam.
The latter always expressed his conviction, that, when the
designs of the enemy became known at Cambridge, Genl.
Ward, instead of witholding succours, pressed forward all
he could with safety, without hazarding a general battle )

Putnam returned again to the hill, but the reinforcement
had not arrived. By this time the enemy's force was em-
barked, and making towards Morton's Point, and he ordered the detachment under Knowlton, with some scattering
troops not employed at the redoubt, to take post at a rail
fence, and extend onward to Mystic River, and make the
best preparation in their power for defence.

Calculating, as Genl. Putnam said he had always done,
that if the enemy came out with a strong force, he must be
ultimately driven from his first position, he was anxious to
form a second rallying point,—that from the beginning he
had this in view, and expected there might have been time
to accomplish it before any serious attack would be made;
but the promptitude of the enemy's movements, and the
delay of the second detachment, had allowed no time.
Still however, he was unwilling wholly to abandon it, and
determined if it were yet possible to make some defences
on Bunker Hill. Here he was busily employed with such
means as were in his power, till the reinforcement arrived,
and almost at the same moment, the enemy advanced slow-
ly in columns, and opened a fire from their field artillery.
He hasted as soon as possible to place all his disposable

force where he judged it most needed, and was proceeding himself to take a position near the centre of the line when Warren met him.

Alluding to a former conversation, he said, "I am sorry to see you here Genl. Warren,—I wish you had taken my advice and left this day to us, for, from appearances, we shall have a sharp time of it, and since you are here, I am ready to submit myself to your orders." Warren replied,— "I came only as a volunteer,—I know nothing of your dispositions, nor will I interfere with them. Tell me where I can be most useful." Putnam pointed to the redoubt, and, intent on his safety, said,—"You will be covered there." ' Don't think," said Warren, "I came here to seek a place of *safety*, but tell me where the onset will be most furious." Putnam pointed again to the redoubt,—"*That*," said he, "is the enemy's object,—Prescott is there, and will do *his* duty, and if it *can* be defended, the day will be ours." Warren left him, and walked quickly towards the redoubt. The rest, alas, is but too well known.

For many reasons I have purposely avoided as much as possible, any allusion to "An Account of the Battle of Bunker Hill," published in 1818. I am now willing to believe it was written under some very great mistake, and that the writer is far more sorry than I *can* be, that he ever touched the subject at all. For, however heart-searching and scorching to my soul that "account" was for a time, I cannot now do otherways than *rejoice* at an occasion which has brought Genl. Putnam out as "gold twice assayed in the furnace," and has also led to a more critical investigation of the history of that battle than had ever before been made,—without which the splendid edifice to be erected in commemoration of it might hardly have been thought of, nor that gratifying spectacle ever been witnessed which, of late, filled so many hearts with gladness.

For other reasons I have withheld a recapitulation of much that I have heard of Genl. Putnam's own doings in that battle. Late as the time is, many of them have been drawn from some of the few survivors who themselves were witnesses of his deeds,—enough to prove that, difficult and arduous as were his duties on that eventful day, they were fearlessly and faithfully performed.

My chief object in making this communication has been to state facts, which from their nature were accessible *at the time* to but few, and which, if they existed as I have detailed them, make it questionable whether, without the agency of Genl. Putnam, the battle of Bunker Hill would ever have been fought

I have no other *direct* authority for the truth of such parts of this statement as purport to come from the mouth of Genl Putnam, than that they were made to me at the time, and often repeated for fifteen years after by him. If they are materially incorrect, he must have related them untruly, or they have been unfairly reported by me For such as were the result of my own observation, or in which I personally bore a very unimportant part, I can say with confidence, that my recollection of them is believed to be as perfect as almost any event of my life. They have till now been kept back from a reluctance to come forward as a volunteer witness in a case where it must be supposed my feelings are interested,—and I regret they should now form so considerable a part of what I have felt it due to my father's memory to disclose. My only apology for introducing them at all is, that they form a connecting link in the chain of my story and have a collateral bearing on the truth of it

If, under other circumstances, I could harbour the base thought of giving even to my Father what was justly due to another, equally brave and honourable, I should certainly be restrained in this instance by the long friendship and high respect I entertain for Judge Prescott, from indulging it against his father. I know too well also, how near of kindred *their* souls were, not to dread for such an act of dishonour the angry frown of Genl. Putnam's spirit, on a son, who, if not a favourite, was always a favoured one. I have no views tending at all to the discredit of Col Prescott, and those who understand them will believe I say this in truth.

Does it take any thing from the glory of Lafayette, who *stormed* the redoubt at Yorktown, that Washington commanded the army? Or, can it take any thing from perhaps the still greater glory of Prescott, who so nobly *defended* his at Charlestown, that another, who *may* have done less than himself, had the general direction of a battle in which he performed a most important part? I know indeed, the cases are not exactly parallel. The army at Yorktown was a regular army, with a known and acknowledged chief, whose right of command no one ever disputed;—that at Cambridge, almost without order, and quite without the discipline so essential to order. But the main question continues the same. Had not Putnam superior rank to Prescott? and has it not been sufficiently demonstrated that he was in the battle, and from beginning to end exercising all the properties of command? Why then, should there be any disposition manifested to place him somewhere *not* in the foreground of the picture?

There may be, and there probably *is* a local feeling on this subject;—but, (I ask the question with great deference,) is it such a feeling as ought to be indulged in this case? Is it a generous, a magnanimous feeling?—such as that which drew Putnam from the quietness of his farm to breast the horrors of a civil war, with the moral certainty of a "halter" if unsuccessful, unless it should have been his happy lot to find death as Warren found it—bravely contending for the liberties of his country! Finally, is it in accordance with that exalted sentiment of Webster's lofty mind —"*Let our object be our Country our whole Country, and nothing but our Country!*"

May HE, "in whose hand our breath is, and whose are

all our ways," incline every heart to the practice of this sound political maxim.

The foregoing statements are now most respectfully submitted to the scrutiny of minds highly discriminating, and I hope they will be judged of, not by preconceived opinions, or under long-indulged prejudices, but by their probability, their consistency, and the general tenour of other information.

> With respectful consideration, I have the honor to be
> > Gentlemen
> > > Your most Obt. and grateful servt.
> > > > DANL. PUTNAM.

Brooklyn Conn., August
1825

CPSIA information can be obtained
at www.ICGtesting.com
Printed in the USA
LVOW03*1048010216

473119LV00010BC/98/P

9 781296 758264